WOMEN IN THE HISPANIC WORLD

WOMEN'S ISSUES:
GLOBAL TRENDS

Women in the Arab World

Women in the World of Japan

Women in the World of Africa

Women in the World of China

Native Women in the Americas

Women in the World of India

Women in the Eastern European World

Women in the World of Southeast Asia

Women in the Hispanic World

Women in the World of Russia

Women in the Mediterranean World

Women in North America's Religious World

WOMEN'S ISSUES:
GLOBAL TRENDS

WOMEN IN THE HISPANIC WORLD

BY
AUTUMN LIBAL

Mason Crest Publishers
Philadelphia

Mason Crest Publishers Inc.
370 Reed Road, Broomall, Pennsylvania 19008
(866) MCP-BOOK (toll free)
www.masoncrest.com

First edition, 2005
13 12 11 10 09 08 07 06 05   10 9 8 7 6 5 4 3 2

Library of Congress Cataloging-in-Publication Data

Libal, Autumn.
   Women in the Hispanic World / by Autumn Libal.
      p. cm. — (Women's issues, global trends)
   Includes index.
         ISBN 1-59084-858-6
         ISBN 1-59084-856-X (series)
   1. Women—Latin America—Juvenile literature. 2. Hispanic American women—Juvenile
literature. I. Title. II. Series.
   HQ1460.5.L5 2005
   305.48'868073—dc22
                     2004011482

Produced by Harding House Publishing Service, Inc.
www.hardinghousepages.com
Interior design by Michelle Bouch and MK Bassett-Harvey.
Illustrations by Michelle Bouch.
Cover design by Benjamin Stewart.
Printed in India.

CONTENTS

INTRODUCTION

by Mary Jo Dudley

The last thirty years have been a time of great progress for women around the world. In some countries, especially where women have more access to education and work opportunities, the relationships between women and men have changed radically. The boundaries between men's roles and women's roles have been crossed, and women are enjoying many experiences that were denied them in past centuries.

But there is still much to be done. On the global stage, women are increasingly the ones who suffer most from poverty. At the same time that they produce 75 to 90 percent of the world's food crops, they are also responsible for taking care of their households. According to the United Nations, in no country in the world do men come anywhere near to spending as much time on housework as women do. This means that women's job opportunities are often extremely limited, contributing to the "feminization of poverty."

In fact, two out of every three poor adults are women. According to the Decade of Women, "Women do two-thirds of the world's work, receive 10 percent of the world's income, and own one percent of the means of production." Women often have no choice but to take jobs that lack long-term security or

adequate pay; many women work in dangerous working conditions or in unprotected home-based industries. This series clearly illustrates how historic events and contemporary trends (such as war, conflicts, and migration) have also contributed to women's loss of property and diminished access to resources.

A recent report from Human Rights Watch indicates that many countries continue to deny women basic legal protections. Amnesty International points out, "Governments are not living up to their promises under the Women's Convention to protect women from discrimination and violence such as rape and female genital mutilation." Many nations—including the United States—have not ratified the United Nations' Women's Treaty.

During times of armed conflict, especially under policies of ethnic cleansing, women are particularly at risk. Murder, torture, systematic rape, forced pregnancy and forced abortions are all too common human rights violations endured by women around the world. This series presents the experience of women in Vietnam, Cambodia, the Middle East, and other war torn regions.

In the political arena, equality between men and women has still not been achieved. Around the world, women are underrepresented in their local and national governments; on average, women represent only 10 percent of all legislators worldwide. This series provides excellent examples of key female leaders who have promoted women's rights and occupied unique leadership positions, despite historical contexts that would normally have shut them out from political and social prominence.

The Fourth World Conference on Women called upon the international community to take action in the following areas of concern:

- the persistent and increasing burden of poverty on women
- inequalities and inadequacies in access to education and training
- inequalities and inadequacies in access to health care and related services
- violence against women

- the effects of armed or other kinds of conflict on women
- inequality in economic structures and policies, in all forms of productive processes, and in access to resources
- insufficient mechanisms at all levels to promote the advancement of women
- lack of protection of women's human rights
- stereotyping of women and inequality in women's participation in all community systems, especially the media
- gender inequalities in the management of natural resources and the safeguarding of the environment
- persistent discrimination against and violation of the rights of female children

The Conference's mission statement includes these sentences: "Equality between women and men is a matter of human rights and a condition for social justice and is also a necessary and fundamental prerequisite for equality, development and peace. . . equality between women and men is a condition . . . for society to meet the challenges of the twenty-first century." This series provides examples of how women have risen above adversity, despite their disadvantaged social, economic, and political positions.

Each book in WOMEN'S ISSUES: GLOBAL TRENDS takes a look at women's lives in a different key region or culture, revealing the history, contributions, triumphs, and challenges of women around the world. Women play key roles in shaping families, spirituality, and societies. By interweaving historic backdrops with the modern-day evolving role of women in the home and in society at large, this series presents the important part women play as cultural communicators. Protection of women's rights is an integral part of universal human rights, peace, and economic security. As a result, readers who gain understanding of women's lives around the world will have deeper insight into the current condition of global interactions.

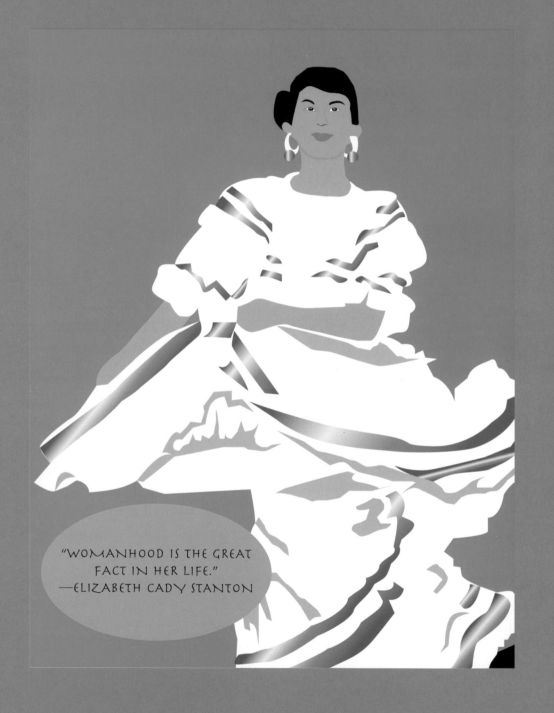

"WOMANHOOD IS THE GREAT
FACT IN HER LIFE."
—ELIZABETH CADY STANTON

LA QUINCEAÑERA: A CELEBRATION OF HISPANIC WOMANHOOD

Alicia lay in bed staring at the ceiling. She took a deep breath and attempted to remain calm. It was difficult with all the commotion in the house. Her mother's clipped, staccato voice rose in urgent tones—probably a last-minute call to the caterer. Alicia counted the bangs as the porch's screen door opened and closed—twenty-two—her father carrying the last of the chairs out to the backyard. She turned her attention to the steady clap of hammers floating through the window—the workmen finishing setting up the stage.

As she listened to these sounds, Alicia contemplated the feeling turning in her stomach. She couldn't explain how she felt. After all, she'd been waiting for this day for years, planning it for months, counting down the days. Last night she'd gone to bed so excited she could barely sleep. But what was this? During the night, some unsuspected interloper had crept through the darkness and invaded her stomach. What was this horrible invader that threatened to ruin everything? Then Alicia realized it was fear—and even more confusing—it was sadness.

Alicia knew she had to get out of bed and dress. Her friends and family would be arriving soon, and everything was supposed to be perfect. This was her special day, but suddenly all the fun, hope, excitement, and sparkle had been drained out of it. What were these tears welling in her eyes and dripping onto her pillow? Alicia just couldn't understand herself.

A tap on the door interrupted her thoughts. "Alicia. Up, up!"

It was her mother. Part of Alicia wanted her mother to come in, talk to her, and soothe her. The other part, however, suddenly felt ashamed. Here the whole family was working hard to make this day the best for her, and all she could do was lie in bed and cry. Before she could decide whether to ask her mother to come in, the sound of three pairs of feet pounded down the hall—her little brothers. Alicia heard her mother go tearing after them, admonishments and oaths punctuating the air.

Ten more minutes ticked by. Alicia looked at the clock. Eight-forty—the service would be starting in less than an hour. She couldn't wait any longer. Alicia grabbed a tissue from the nightstand, dried her eyes, dragged herself from bed, and began to dress.

When she stood in front of the mirror, her skirt billowed out like a pink satin cloud, and sparkling beads dripped from her ears. She swept her hair up, pinned it, and attached little flowers. The hairstyle made her look very adult, and for some reason this made the tears start anew. Alicia watched as the teardrops plopped onto the pink satin, creating dark splotches on the dress, which just made her cry even harder.

An exclamation from behind jolted Alicia from her stupor. Alicia turned. Her mother had entered the bedroom unnoticed, and now she was standing looking almost as distraught as Alicia felt.

"Alicia, what's wrong?"

It was more than Alicia could bear. She ran across the room, pink satin bouncing around her, and collapsed sobbing into her mother's arms. All the

A young Latina girl may be part of both the modern world and the traditional past.

Latino people love to celebrate life's special occasions.

WOMEN IN THE HISPANIC WORLD

conflicting feelings that had been warring inside of her suddenly bubbled out in a rush.

"Everything's gone wrong," Alicia cried into her mother's shoulder. "I was supposed to be so happy . . . I was so happy . . . but now I'm just so sad. It's like everything is changing so fast. I couldn't wait for today to come, and now it's here, and tonight it will be over, and everything will be different, and all I'll have to look forward to is getting married, and I'm scared."

Alicia hadn't realized she felt all these things, but as they poured from her lips, she knew they were true. It suddenly felt good to be cradled in her mother's arms as if she was a little girl again, and she didn't want to move.

"Oh, *mi hija*," her mother spoke. Alicia thought she heard a small smile in her mother's voice. "Crying on your own *quinceañera*? Come sit."

Alicia allowed herself to be towed to the foot of the bed and obediently sat down. With a gentle hand, her mother lifted Alicia's chin until their eyes met.

"Alicia, you are right. Everything changes. We all get older. You are no longer a child. But Alicia, the important things, they always stay the same. Today we celebrate that you are a woman, but you are still Alicia. You are still our daughter. We are still your family. It's a happy day, a day of celebration. It might seem like something is ending, but it is also the start of something new and wonderful." She paused, and when she spoke again, a hint of laughter crept into her voice. "And Alicia, this is not your grandmother's quinceañera. No one is going to be marrying you off tomorrow! There will be plenty more years to think about that!"

Now Alicia couldn't help but smile too. Satisfied, her mother took her hand and stood up, "Now no more crying. Come put on some makeup. You have a big party to go to."

L*a quinceañera*, the celebration of a girl's fifteenth birthday, is a tradition many Hispanic girls look forward to for years. On this special day, the girl dresses in a beautiful pink, white, or pastel gown and is attended by as many as fourteen female and fourteen male friends.

The big day begins with a church service, an intimate ceremony that's generally only for family and close friends. There is usually a special portion of the service when the priest speaks to the girl about what it means to be a woman. After the church service, the quinceañera crowd swells as the girl's other guests arrive for a dinner, followed by a dance.

Quinceañeras can be small affairs or huge parties, depending on how much money a family can afford to spend on their daughter's big day. For many Hispanic girls, it is a day they look forward to and plan for weeks, months, or even years beforehand.

In the past, the quinceañera symbolized a girl's entrance into womanhood. Today, the quinceañera has taken on additional meaning, especially in the United States. Crime, drugs, gangs, teen pregnancy, and other social difficulties are prevalent in some parts of America. In areas facing these problems, the quinceañera has become a celebration of "making it" through these dangers and reaching womanhood safe, alive, and (parents hope) virtuous.

WOMEN IN THE HISPANIC WORLD

Hispanic women may be well-to-do and sophisticated . . .

. . . or wear clothes made by hand from bright Native fabrics.

WOMEN IN THE HISPANIC WORLD

So why would Alicia be feeling sad on a day so many girls look forward to? The quinceañera is much more than just a birthday party, and Alicia's sadness is related to the change the quinceañera is ushering into her life. A quinceañera symbolizes a girl's entrance into womanhood. Traditionally, the quinceañera celebrated the preservation of the girl's virginity and announced her readiness for marriage. Today, the quinceañera can mean different things for different people, but the emphasis on the transition from girlhood to womanhood remains the same.

Some aspects of the quinceañera may vary. For example, a Mexican girl's quinceañera celebration may be somewhat different from a Cuban girl's celebration. Many aspects of this tradition, however, are seen *cross-culturally*. For many girls today, the quinceañera may seem like just a great celebration or party in her honor, but it is really much more than that. In the eyes of her community, the girl is forever changed. She is now an adult. More specifically, she is now a woman.

But what does it mean to be a woman, and what is unique about Hispanic womanhood? To answer these questions, we need to understand more about Hispanic culture as a whole and the differences between men and women in Latino society.

"SNOWFLAKES, LEAVES, HUMANS, PLANTS, RAINDROPS, STARS, MOLECULES, MICROSCOPIC ENTITIES ALL COME IN COMMUNITIES. THE SINGULAR CAN-NOT IN REALITY EXIST."
—PAULA GUNN ALLEN

WHAT'S IN A NAME?
UNDERSTANDING THE TERM
"HISPANIC"

Jennifer felt horribly confused. Did she and Raquel have a fight? Jennifer wasn't sure. It was all so complicated. They had just left social studies class when it happened. Raquel was fuming, and at first Jennifer didn't understand why. Raquel angrily enlightened her.

"Can you believe that Mr. Robins?" Raquel raged. "How many times do I have to tell him that we're not Hispanic, we're Latina. I swear, the next time he says something like that I'm going to the school board. He's plain *racist*."

Jennifer, however, didn't see why Raquel wanted to make trouble. "Oh, come on. It's not that big of a deal," Jennifer said without thinking. The moment the words left her lips, however, she knew it was the wrong thing to say.

"Not that big of a deal!" Raquel threw Jennifer's words back at her. "Not that big of a deal?"

"Well," Jennifer stammered, trying to explain herself, "who cares what they call us? It's not like we're all the same anyway."

Raquel stared at Jennifer first with disbelief, then with anger. Her eyes narrowed, and when she finally spoke her voice was venomous.

Some Hispanic women prefer the term "Latina".

"Look, Jennifer," she spat, "we're all in this together, and if we don't unite, nothing's going to change. Girl, you better figure out who your real friends are, or you're never going to make it in this country." With that, Raquel stalked away.

Jennifer stood alone and perplexed. She'd listened to Raquel rail against the word "Hispanic" many times. Raquel's favorite saying was, "If you accept their name for you, then you accept that they have power over you." Jennifer just didn't see why it was such a big deal. If people wanted to call her Hispanic, fine. She knew who she was—a proud Puerto Rican girl. Raquel was her best friend, but Raquel wasn't Puerto Rican. She was Mexican American, so her insistence that they unite under the banner "Latina" made little more sense to Jennifer than the *Anglos'* insistence on calling her Hispanic.

Then Jennifer thought about the racism in America and the many barriers to Mexican Americans', Puerto Ricans', Nicaraguans', and other "Hispanic" peoples' success. Jennifer knew that as females, she and Raquel would have an especially hard time overcoming *discrimination* and *stereotypes*. Maybe Raquel was right. After all, didn't the Americans love to say, "United we stand. Divided we fall"? Maybe, if they were going to overcome the many hardships facing them, all the people from *Latin America* would have to unite as one community, but what did it matter if they called themselves Hispanic or Latina?

Jennifer, a Puerto Rican girl in America, is struggling with questions concerning her identity. Identity is the way you see yourself and others, and it is made up of many factors. For example, gender, whether you are female or male, is a fundamental form of identity. Things like *ethnicity*, religion, and nationality also play a large role in identity. In one's teenage years, questions concerning identity can become especially perplexing as one tries to understand oneself and others. Understanding one's family history and *cultural* background usually helps a person form her sense of identity.

Jennifer and Raquel are struggling to understand how the term "Hispanic" fits into their individual identities. Hispanic is a term given to a certain *linguistic* group; it is a label for a type of group identity. In North America, people usually use the word Hispanic to describe any person who is descended from Spanish-speaking ancestors but does not come from Spain. This definition, however, includes many different groups of people from numerous countries. The United States has a large Spanish-speaking population, and many countries in the Americas have Spanish as their official language. Those countries are Mexico, the Central American countries of Guatemala, El Salvador, Honduras, Nicaragua, Costa Rica, and Panama, the Caribbean countries of Cuba and Dominican Republic, and the South American countries of Venezuela, Colombia, Ecuador, Peru, Bolivia, Paraguay, Uruguay, Argentina, and Chile. Spanish is also the first language of Puerto Rico, which is a *protectorate* of the United States.

These regions, of course, did not always speak Spanish. In the 1400s, the people of Spain were the first in a great wave of Europeans to come to the Americas. The Spanish *conquistadors*, as they are often called, eventually claimed huge portions of land in the Caribbean and South, Central, and North America. In general, the conquest of the Americas was a brutal takeover of the Native peoples who already lived here. Millions of people throughout the Americas were killed by the wars, poverty, and diseases the Europeans brought.

The first Spanish conquistadors and settlers were men. They generally came looking for riches, like gold. Some of these men married Native women and had families. These Spanish settlers were now in a land very different from their home, and they adopted Native practices and ways of life that were more suited to this land than their own traditional ways. Meanwhile, immigration from Spain increased, with whole families now settling in the Americas. Many people came as missionaries to convert the Native people to Christianity. The

Many Americans have Hispanic backgrounds.

Spanish people (and later other Europeans) also brought slaves from Africa. These various African cultures further influenced the Spanish settlers and their descendants. Over hundreds of years, new cultures developed that combined aspects of Spanish, Native, and African heritages and responded to changing conditions in the Americas.

Today, although Spanish is the official language of many American countries and regions, it would be wrong to call their citizens Spanish. Spanish-speaking people in the Americas have a very different heritage and culture than people have in Spain. In fact, many Spanish-speaking people in the Americas today would have to trace their ancestry back hundreds of years to find a link with Spain. Others have no Spanish link at all (except for the language that they speak). To call everyone who speaks the Spanish language "Spanish" would make no more sense than calling all English-speaking Americans "English." In the 1980s, the U.S. government developed the term "Hispanic" to describe anyone in the Americas who spoke Spanish as their first language or had Spanish heritage.

The term "Hispanic" is generally only used in the United States and Canada, and it has been problematic from the beginning. As you saw in Jennifer and Raquel's argument, not everyone likes the name. There are a number of reasons for this. One reason is that many people don't appreciate the U.S. government labeling them. They would rather define their own identities than have a government body define their identity for them. The Americas are a huge and diverse place. Because "Hispanic" is a linguistic grouping, it includes people of many different nationalities, ethnicities, races, and cultural backgrounds, and many people don't like the way the term Hispanic lumps everyone together. Furthermore, many people from the Americas have mixed ancestry. Some people, therefore, resent the term Hispanic because it emphasizes Spanish heritage without acknowledging other aspects of their backgrounds.

This mother and daughter from Central America also speak Spanish as their first language.

A South American woman.

Hispanic people have lived in North America for generations. For example, much of the southwestern United States was annexed from Mexico, and many Hispanic communities suddenly became part of America. Other Hispanic people have come to North America as immigrants, often fleeing poverty or war in their native countries.

In Jennifer and Raquel's story, Raquel wants to be called Latina instead of Hispanic. Latina is the feminine form of the term Latino. (Unlike English, the Spanish language assigns a gender to most nouns and adjectives. For example, in English, the word "friend" has no gender. In Spanish, however, the word for a female friend is *amiga*, while the word for a male friend is *amigo*.) Many Latin American people living in the United States and Canada today prefer the term Latino to Hispanic. The term Latino incorporates Latin American people from multiple backgrounds rather than separating out people of Spanish descent. Though Spanish is spoken by a majority of people in Latin America, other languages are also spoken. For example, Portuguese is the official language of Brazil, and French is the official language of French Guiana. Portuguese and

GETTING THE BLAME

Many of America's immigrants are Hispanic, and they often get blamed for economic difficulties. Some states, like California, have passed laws barring many illegal immigrants from social services like health care and public education. But even illegal immigrants may give more to communities and economies than they take. For example, immigrants often work in difficult, low-paying, and dangerous jobs that other Americans won't take. Lower wages and safety standards for workers mean higher profits for companies and cheaper goods and services for consumers. Immigrants, both legal and illegal, become a major backbone for the economy. Many people in America benefit at the expense of these low-wage workers. Not only are these workers not thanked for their hard labor and sacrifice, they are actually blamed for America's problems—a situation that hardly seems fair. As scholar Geoffrey Fox states in his book **Hispanic Nation**: "Immigrants create more wealth than they consume and contribute far more in taxes than they cost."

A woman from Guatemala displays her weaving.

French speakers are not considered Hispanic, but they are considered Latino. Some Mexican Americans prefer the term Chicano (a name that used to be an insult but that some have reclaimed as a term of pride). Most people, however, would rather not be called any of these names. They prefer to be identified by

Many Puerto Ricans live in New York City and other areas of mainland United States.

their individual nationalities—as Mexican, Puerto Rican, Cuban, or Chilean, for example—than lumped together as a group.

Despite these disagreements and the diversity of Spanish-speaking people in the Americas, some cultural aspects are shared across groups, and the term

"Hispanic" can be useful. The idea of a unique and *cohesive* Hispanic culture has flourished in North America. Although people in Central America, South America, or the Caribbean generally don't call themselves Hispanic, many people in North America adopt the term as part of their identities. In a land where the majority of people speak English, Spanish speakers often join together, forming strong communities, supporting one another, and emphasizing cultural similarities. In this way, a larger Hispanic culture solidifies, despite the fact that the members of that culture may come from different countries and have different backgrounds. As Jennifer stated, Hispanic citizens and immigrants can face a huge amount of racism and barriers to their advancement in the United States. Commitment to Hispanic community and culture can help people deal with these hardships. Furthermore, Hispanic culture is prevalent in the *media*. Every day, television, music, radio, books, leaders, and other influential people help define and reinforce that culture.

Today, the Spanish language and Hispanic culture are important parts of North American culture. Hispanic people stand on the brink of becoming the United States' largest minority and are already the majority population of some cities. Spanish appears on everything from street signs to nutrition labels. Thousands of Spanish words, like *cafeteria, patio, canyon, taco,* and *mosquito,* have been adopted into English. Salsa, tango, merengúe, and other forms of music and dance entertain both Hispanic and non-Hispanic people. Hispanic foods are enjoyed in millions of North American homes, and Hispanic artists, actors, musicians, athletes, *activists*, and other high-profile individuals enrich all of our lives.

Jennifer and Raquel's story, however, is not simply about questioning their Hispanic identity. Jennifer is struggling with another issue as well. The story states, "Jennifer knew that, as females, she and Raquel would have an especially hard time overcoming discrimination and stereotypes." Why should Jennifer think that things would be more difficult for her as a female?

Being a Hispanic woman can mean different things.

Jennifer's belief comes from the fact that Hispanic culture (like cultures all over the world) regards girls and boys as different. This means that an individual's experience growing up Hispanic will be different depending on whether the person is a girl or a boy. Right or wrong, individuals face different attitudes,

WOMEN IN THE HISPANIC WORLD

challenges, and opportunities depending on their gender, and these differences reflect cultural attitudes toward the sexes.

In this book, we explore what it means to be a Hispanic woman. Although the term "Hispanic" is generally only used in North America, we will consider Spanish-speaking women's lives in Central America, South America, and the Caribbean as well.

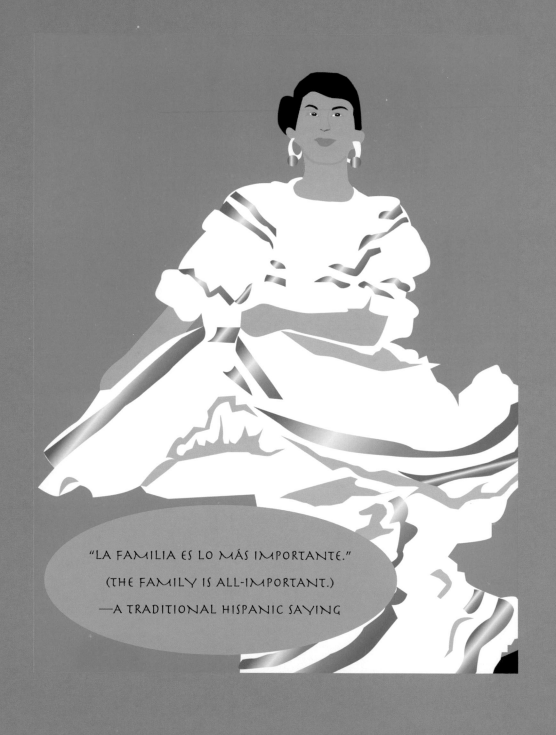

"LA FAMILIA ES LO MÁS IMPORTANTE."
(THE FAMILY IS ALL-IMPORTANT.)
—A TRADITIONAL HISPANIC SAYING

HISPANIC WOMEN THROUGHOUT HISTORY

Maria was only twenty-four, but she already felt old. She had struggled all her life. At three, she toddled beside her mother on the coffee plantation, crawling beneath the plants to find shade as the hours wore away. Maria was barely five when she, too, began picking the little red beans, adding her own tiny hands to the family's daily labor.

At home, there never seemed to be enough food, and Maria's father and two brothers got the best of everything. Maria, her four sisters, and her mother were always hungry, but they never complained.

Maria's brothers had been loud and boisterous. Each day, Maria watched from a distance as the boys kicked up dirt on their way home from school. Mama's kisses always greeted them at the door. Then they ran into the yard to get sweaty playing games. Maria couldn't remember ever playing this way. Her memories were all of household chores, picking coffee, spinning wool into yarn, and butchering and plucking chickens.

Now Maria's own daughters were performing many of the chores and killing and plucking the chickens, but there was still always work for Maria to do. She

had given birth to five children. Only three had survived, but even these three were difficult to support. Life with her husband had been hard. Faced with his aggressive nature, Maria had always felt nervous and remained quiet. At the same time, she had been deeply thankful for her husband. He was hardworking and provided for the children, but like so many others, he died in the mines. Maria knew her family would help her if they could, but her sisters and brothers all had children of their own. Maria just didn't know how she was going to feed these three little mouths by herself.

Like women all over the world, throughout history Hispanic women's lives have been defined by hard work. Maria's life displays many of the conditions and challenges that Hispanic women faced in Latin and North America. Women were generally considered inferior to men in Hispanic culture. Their activities were largely limited to their homes, and they had to be *subservient* to their husbands. Parents valued the birth of boys over the birth of girls, and boys often received better treatment from both their parents than girls received.

A Hispanic woman's daily routine was typical for women of her times. She woke early each morning to stoke the household fire, pump water from a well or fetch it from another source, grind corn, wheat, or other grains into flour, and prepare the morning meal. Unlike today when we can turn on a tap for water, run to the store for bread, and put leftovers in the refrigerator to reheat for tomorrow's meal, in times past the job of feeding a family began from scratch every day. The never-ending cycle of food preparation, however, was only one of a woman's many labors. Making yarn, cloth, clothing, and blankets was another major task. Spinning, weaving, and sewing were essential skills that women used to keep their families clothed and warm, and these skills were learned and practiced from a very young age. At just five years old, girls would already be learning certain skills and performing small tasks. By the time a girl was twelve, she knew how to run a household.

This girl from South America already has many household responsibilities.

Peruvian women and children.

A Hispanic girl's household management skills were employed relatively early in her life when she married and began her own family. Parents chose their children's marriage partners and expected their children to accept this decision. Most women and men in North American society today choose highly independent life paths, and their personal desires play a large role in their decisions. This social attitude, however, that values an individual's desires is a relatively recent phenomenon. Traditional Hispanic society considered the family much more important than the individual, and most people felt great pressure to fulfill their expected social roles. A woman was expected to devote herself completely to her husband and children, sacrifice her own feelings and desires, and endure hardship for her family.

One reason Hispanic culture valued the family above all else was because families generally supported themselves through agriculture. To grow food and raise animals, a family needed land. Unlike other societies around the world, however, the Hispanic family rarely divided its land among its members, a practice that could eventually cause the *dissolution* of the family and its wealth. Instead, large extended families cooperated, farming the land they held in common. Poverty always threatened, as one bad harvest or natural disaster could wipe out a whole year's labor and resources. Everyone in the family needed to work and support each other, and *individualism* was highly discouraged.

Hispanic society was traditionally patriarchal and patrilocal, meaning that family authority was vested in the head male and that when a couple married, they went to live with the husband's side of the family. In the past, Hispanic women married very young, usually around fifteen years old. Upon marriage, a woman generally left her childhood home to live in her husband's house. Ties between families related by marriage were often very strong.

Besides her husband, the most important person in a new bride's life was her mother-in-law. Moving in with her husband usually meant moving in with his parents, grandparents, his brothers and their wives, his unmarried sisters, and his nieces and nephews. Women were a powerful force within Hispanic families, and the most senior woman could have a lot of control over other members of the household. Though the patriarch was the supreme authority figure of a family, his wife directed all the work within the house, and all the women of the house were subject to her will and obeyed her direction.

Hispanic culture valued large families. Fewer children survived until adulthood than do today, so women often gave birth to many more children than would survive. Agricultural societies needed many hands to work, and children provided extra labor. Children were also a couple's guarantee of support in their old age. Furthermore, modern forms of birth control did not exist, and social and religious values generally discouraged other forms of family planning. These values declared that women should welcome all the children with whom God chose to bless them, regardless of God's timing. The result was large families with children spaced close together.

MACHISMO: REALITY OR MYTH

One aspect of Hispanic society that has received a lot of attention, much of which is negative, is the concept of machismo. Machismo is often blamed for women's inferior status in Hispanic society. Many people disagree, however, on what machismo is, whether it exists at all, and what impact it has on Hispanic women's lives.

Machismo is often defined as excessive masculinity or aggressive male pride. In Hispanic societies, as in many other societies in the world, certain qualities like physical strength, aggressiveness, *assertiveness*, and bravery were associated with men. Things like physical and mental weakness, selflessness, emotionality, and fear were associated with women. Since men were seen as superior to women, "male qualities" were generally seen as superior to "female qualities." A man who could cultivate all his strong, male qualities and banish

A husband and wife in Central America.

any female qualities from his *persona* was a manly man, a macho man; he had machismo.

Personal and family pride, honor, and respectability were extremely important in Hispanic society, and this may be one reason why men sought and valued machismo. However, many people, both Hispanic and non-Hispanic, feel

Many Latina women are taught to be subservient to the man in their lives.

WOMEN IN THE HISPANIC WORLD

that the quest for machismo led to the further *subjugation* of women in Hispanic society. One of the easiest ways for a man to demonstrate his super-masculinity—or machismo—was to display complete control over his family. Many women and children suffered under their husbands', fathers', brothers', and sons' aggressive behavior, which was reinforced, *sanctioned*, and *perpetuated* by the larger society.

Today, stereotypes about Hispanic men and machismo abound. It is important to remember that not all Hispanic men valued or displayed machismo. In fact, some scholars today think machismo was far less influential in Hispanic society than many people believe. For example, although women were expected

Que bueno que tuvo niña primero para que ella le ayude con los de más niños. (It's good your first-born is a girl. She'll be able to help you with the other children you will have.)
—a traditional Hispanic saying to comfort mothers when their first-born is a girl

to be loyal, obedient, and subservient to their husbands, Hispanic society also valued and demanded respect for women, especially for mothers.

Despite social values that treated women as inferior to men, Hispanic women were influential in many ways. In many households, women oversaw the family's daily work, finances, and investments. Furthermore, Hispanic society has a long tradition of female-headed households. As in many societies, Hispanic men had a lower life expectancy than women, were often employed in dangerous occupations like mining or the military, and were more likely than women to leave their families. Many women became the heads of their households when their husbands died or left.

Traditional Hispanic society encouraged women to stay in the home, but circumstances often required women to work. Though middle- and upper-class women could afford to live by the strict social values that kept them in their kitchens and tending to their children, the many lower class families needed every able body earning money. Furthermore, as we saw in chapter 1, Hispanic society is incredibly *diverse*, and circumstances change from place to place. In some places, women (at least from the upper classes) had more opportunities for education and employment than women had in other areas. In Chile, for example, women have been attending medical school and becoming doctors since the late 1870s. Nevertheless, these women still faced discrimination in their field and were often given the title of "pharmacist" even though they had the full qualifications of a medical doctor.

Hispanic women were also influential in the public sphere. Although historically, Hispanic women did not have as many legal rights as men (for example, in most Latin-American countries, women did not receive the right to vote until the 1930s, '40s, and '50s) and could not serve in public office, they found other ways to make their voices heard, often using their positions as wives and mothers to gain and exert influence in their communities and in

politics. Many women in Hispanic society have embarked on important and sometimes dangerous work on behalf of themselves, their families, and their communities. You will read about some of these amazing women throughout the remainder of this book. First, however, we'll look at what Hispanic women's lives are like today.

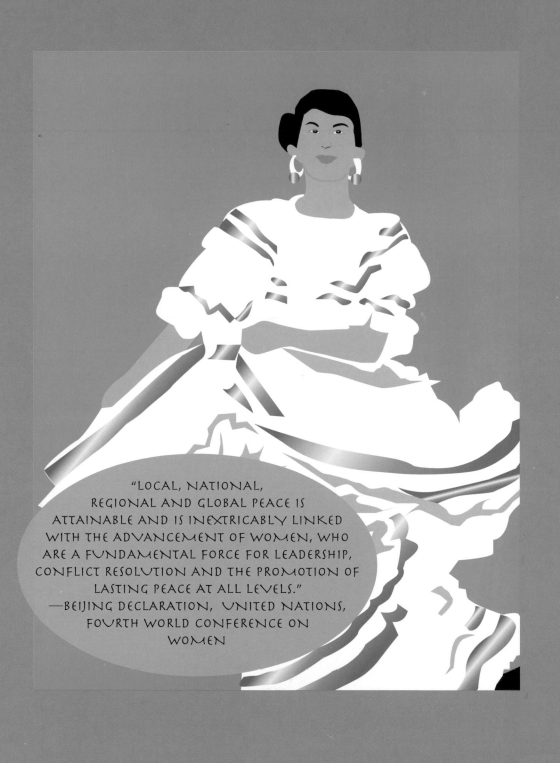

"LOCAL, NATIONAL, REGIONAL AND GLOBAL PEACE IS ATTAINABLE AND IS INEXTRICABLY LINKED WITH THE ADVANCEMENT OF WOMEN, WHO ARE A FUNDAMENTAL FORCE FOR LEADERSHIP, CONFLICT RESOLUTION AND THE PROMOTION OF LASTING PEACE AT ALL LEVELS."
—BEIJING DECLARATION, UNITED NATIONS, FOURTH WORLD CONFERENCE ON WOMEN

4

HISPANIC WOMEN TODAY: EDUCATION, THE ECONOMY, AND POLITICS

Focus on women's circumstances around the world has increased greatly in recent years. In the last three decades, many members of the international community began to see women's advancement and equality as a top priority for the world. To this end, global efforts have been made at improving women's situations in education, health, society, the economy, and government.

The United Nations has worked at the heart of these global efforts. In 1979, a huge step toward equal rights for women was made in something called the Convention on the Elimination of All Forms of Discrimination Against Women (CEDAW). Many people call the CEDAW "an international bill of rights for women." This is a very good description. The CEDAW is an international treaty that demands an end to all forms of discrimination against women. Once a country has accepted the treaty, it is required to act according to the treaty's principals, put laws into place to protect women and ensure their equality, and submit reports on their progress at least every four years. The

United Nations' Web site lists three of the main responsibilities countries take on by accepting CEDAW. They are:

1. To incorporate the principle of equality of men and women in their legal system, abolish all discriminatory laws, and adopt appropriate ones prohibiting discrimination against women.

2. To establish tribunals and other public institutions to ensure the effective protection of women against discrimination.

3. To ensure elimination of all acts of discrimination against women by persons, organizations, or enterprises.

To date, every Spanish-speaking country in the Americas has accepted CEDAW (the United States is one of the only countries in the world that has not), and most have been party to the convention since 1980. However, this does not mean that gender equality has been achieved for all Hispanic women. Countries have varying levels of commitment to the agreement, and many countries lack the resources to implement all the changes CEDAW requires. Political upheaval and *civil* strife have sapped some area's resources. In some places, efforts toward advancing women's rights have fallen (at least temporarily) by the wayside in the wake of other, sometimes violent, struggles.

Lawmakers can sign conventions and governments can proclaim new attitudes, but populations are often slow to change their ways—especially when it comes to something as deeply ingrained as discrimination against women. In some countries, the official laws have changed, but actual practices have not. Even in countries that have been committed to gender equality for decades, challenges still persist. Some women may not even be aware that there are laws forbidding things like gender discrimination in hiring. Even when women do

An elderly woman from South America.

This woman makes her living selling flowers.

know their rights, they often have no one to appeal to if those rights have been violated.

Despite these facts, today's Hispanic women are active in every level of society and work in every field. From performers like Gloria Estefan and Jennifer Lopez to scientists like Ellen Ochoa (the first Hispanic female astronaut), Hispanic women are achieving great things. Nevertheless, in some cases Hispanic women's own culture continues to be a barrier to their advancement. Other conditions, like poverty, limited access to education, discrimination in employment, and lack of political representation, continue to affect Hispanic communities in general and Hispanic women in particular.

HISPANIC WOMEN IN EDUCATION

In times past, fewer Hispanic girls attended school than boys. Before countries developed extensive public education systems with easily *accessible* schools, education could be extremely costly. Families who wanted to educate their children often needed to hire private tutors or send their children to boarding schools in other towns. Many families needed their children to stay home and work. Since girls were expected to get married and raise children, many parents didn't see the sense in spending money on a girl's education. Furthermore, few parents were willing to send a girl to a town far from home where the family could not watch and protect her. Of course, many families could not afford to send their sons to school either, or they only had enough money to educate one child. If a family could only choose one child for an education, they would usually choose a boy.

Today, Hispanic girls' access to education is very different. Most countries have expanded their educational systems and have more public schools. Laws now require that all children attend school for a minimum number of years. In countries like Argentina, Colombia, Cuba, El Salvador, Uruguay, and

Venezuela, more women actually go on to higher education than do men. In Bolivia, Ecuador, El Salvador, Guatemala, Mexico, Panama, Paraguay, Peru, and Venezuela, however, women continue to have lower *literacy* rates than men. Most of the *disparity* between women's and men's literacy rates is probably accounted for by the older generations, with the younger generations having more educational equality.

In the United States, the public education system is failing Hispanic communities in many ways. According to a recent study by the American Association of University Women, Hispanic women continue to receive less education than women of other groups. At 30 percent, Hispanic women's dropout rates are significantly higher than white and black women's dropout rates, which are 8.2 and 12.9 percent, respectively. Hispanic women also have a much lower attendance at the college level, although more Hispanic women attend college than Hispanic men. The American Association of University Women believes that the U.S. educational system isn't doing enough to make school accessible and relevant to Hispanic students. Few Hispanic teachers mean few role models, and nationwide, curriculums have almost no material that is specific to Hispanic history, experience, and culture.

Language barriers can also cause significant educational difficulties, especially for Hispanic students who are *first-generation* immigrants. Can you imagine how difficult it would be to attend classes taught in a language you don't understand? By the time students in this situation know the language well enough to succeed in school, they may have already fallen so far behind or become so frustrated with school that they can't catch up. Hispanic girls also tend to have more household responsibilities, such as caring for younger brothers, sisters, and cousins, than girls of other groups. Few schools have options to help girls in these circumstances, such as flexible class schedules, *leniency* for missed classes, or alternatives for students who can't complete their homework on deadline.

A teacher in a Hispanic school.

The American Association of University Women also cites boyfriends, peers, and family members as holding some Hispanic women back from education. Some people accuse those with higher education of becoming "too white." Similarly, some boyfriends will discourage their girlfriends from putting too much effort into school because they don't want a girlfriend or wife

Latina women work in many different jobs.

who is more educated than they are. Furthermore, in some areas of North America, young people need to leave their homes and move to other towns if they want to attend college. Hispanic families sometimes discourage their daughters from leaving home. Poverty, early marriage, pregnancy, and a desire to enter the workforce are other major contributing factors to women's lack of education.

The news, however, is certainly not all bad. Even though their participation in education is still lower than that of women in other groups, Hispanic women's enrollment in colleges and universities has been steadily increasing for decades and will continue to increase in the future.

HISPANIC WOMEN IN THE ECONOMY

Weavings, embroidered clothing, intricately designed blankets, beaded jewelry, cigars, coffee, chocolate—each time you come in contact with one of these things, you may be handling or benefiting from a Hispanic woman's hard work. But these more traditional jobs for women are by no means the only employment opportunities for Hispanic women. In fact, modern Hispanic women participate in every level of the economy. From home-based, family-run businesses to heading huge corporations, Hispanic women are finding success in the world economy like never before.

Today, women make up more than one-third of the adult labor force in almost all Spanish-speaking countries. However, women continue to earn lower wages than men. According to the Pan American Health Organization, urban women's earnings in Spanish-speaking countries range from 55 to 83 percent of what men earn, with the average for all the countries being about 68 percent of what men earn. In fact, there is a *correlation* between the movement toward higher salaries in a given position and a decline in the number of women employed in that field. This problem plagues women into their futures, as lower salaries also mean women get less of a pension when they retire.

Woman will always be dependent until she holds a purse of her own.

—Elizabeth Cady Stanton

Sometimes women earn these lower wages even when they are performing the same work and have the same level of education as men. In most cases, however, women's lower wages occur because women have less access to higher-paying jobs. Despite the few women who have broken into high-powered careers, most Hispanic women continue to work in low-paying, low-*prestige* jobs in industries like food production, cloth- and garment-making, and factory work.

As we saw earlier, however, Hispanic women in many countries actually achieve more education than men. Why, then, do they continue to be employed in low-paying jobs? This situation is called underemployment, and many educated women around the world experience it. Although women now have more education than ever before, men continue to control managerial positions and hiring. Discrimination in hiring, wages, and promotion are still common. Though numerous women are professionally employed, few can get the promotions offered to men. This problem happens in numerous countries all over the

world and is often referred to as the glass ceiling, meaning that women can see how to advance in their employment, have fulfilled all the requirements for that advancement, are capable of holding the job, yet find an invisible barrier separating them from the men at the top.

The Mothers of the Plaza de Mayo of Argentina.

Some of the men in charge of hiring continue to have discriminatory attitudes toward women. They may think that women are not capable of performing a given job. More often, however, employers—even some female employers—assume that women are not worth hiring because they will just get married, have children, and leave their jobs. Women also have more difficulty than men in securing loans to start their own businesses. Often banks refuse to give loans to women, and male *entrepreneurs* are hesitant to do business with women.

HISPANIC WOMEN IN POLITICS

Though Hispanic women's participation on national political scenes is low, their participation in and leadership of *grassroots* organizations is very high. This work generally focuses on issues like poverty, safety, and human rights.

One very famous example of women's political activity in Latin America is the Mothers of the Plaza de Mayo of Argentina. The movement began in the 1970s when Argentina was controlled by a brutal military regime. Anyone who disagreed with the government "disappeared," which usually meant they were murdered and their bodies secretly buried (some of the Mothers of the Plaza de Mayo also "disappeared"). For nearly twenty-five years, women who lost loved ones demonstrated weekly to learn the fates of their children, spouses, and other relatives. These women knew their loved ones were almost certainly dead, but they wanted the Argentine government and military to admit the crimes they committed to their own citizens and to the world. The women never did receive confirmation from the government of what they knew to be their loved ones' fates, but they marched on for decades to keep the memory of the struggle of their loved one's alive.

A similar political movement took place in Chile in the same period, when Augusto Pinochet ruled Chile as a dictator from 1973 until 1990. Pinochet's military force committed *atrocities* against the Chileans. Thousands of

Currently, countries that achieve 30 percent representation for women in political bodies are considered to be doing very well. Today, only two Spanish-speaking countries have achieved this goal. In Argentina, women make up 31 percent of the parliament, while in Costa Rica they make up 35 percent of the parliament. In comparison to countries like the United States and Canada, which have 14 and 21 percent women in Congress and Parliament, respectively, Argentina and Costa Rica are ahead of the curve. Throughout the world, however, many women today are questioning why they should be satisfied with only 30 percent participation when they make up more than 50 percent of the world's population.

Chileans were arrested for their political views, and some were tortured and murdered. No one could speak out against the government's activities for fear of falling victim to the same terrible fate. Despite the dangers, a group of brave Chilean women began challenging Pinochet's regime. The women protested

and documented Pinochet's human rights abuses by sewing arilleras (traditional Chilean tapestries) that depicted the injustices the Chilean people suffered. They sold these handmade memorials to earn income for their oppressed communities. But how could these women get away with their political *dissidence* when others were arrested or even killed for disagreeing with the government? In their book *Modern Latin America*, authors Thomas E. Skidmore and Peter H. Smith speculate that these women were able to protest and *advocate* for change because they did so within traditional gender norms—as wives, mothers, daughters, sisters, and grandmothers—not as workers, activists, leaders, revolutionaries, politicians, or any other roles that were traditionally reserved for men and that were threatening to Pinochet's government. Some women were among those arrested and killed by the Chilean military, but it may be that the military was reluctant to harm "good women" (devoted wives and mothers), who Hispanic culture dictated must be respected.

Considerable resistance to women's participation in political matters continues to be experienced in many places. Members of the group Sendero Luminoso murdered María Elena Moyano, the deputy mayor of a Peruvian *shantytown*. María was a political activist who believed in the power of nonviolence. Unlike Sendero Luminoso, which believed Peru needed an armed revolution, Maria believed Peru needed reform, cooperation among disagreeing parties, and empowerment of all people, especially the poor and women. She was just one of many female leaders that Sendero Luminoso labeled as traitors and killed.

Although all these women took political action in dramatic ways in the face of dangerous circumstances, many other Hispanic women today participate in politics in far more conventional ways. Women are members of *parliament* in every Spanish-speaking country, although their numbers continue to be far lower than their percentage of the population. Furthermore, Hispanic women have finally broken their way into some of the United States' most important

Dr. Antonia Novello, Surgeon General of the United States.

political offices and bodies. In 1990, for example, Antonia Novello, M.D., was appointed as the first female and the first Hispanic Surgeon General of the United States. Today, Loretta and Linda Sanchez both serve as Representatives for California in the U.S. Congress. Two of seven children from a Mexican immigrant family, they are the first sisters to serve in Congress.

"OLD-FASHIONED WAYS WHICH
NO LONGER APPLY TO CHANGED
CONDITIONS ARE A SNARE IN WHICH THE
FEET OF WOMEN HAVE ALWAYS BECOME
READILY ENTANGLED."
—JANE ADDAMS

5

FAMILY LIFE
FOR HISPANIC WOMEN TODAY

Ana had mixed feelings about returning home for summer break. On the one hand, she knew it should be great. There would be the usual big family gathering filled with laughter, food, and the latest gossip. Her parents would express their pride over and over, telling everyone about her good grades at college. She'd get together with friends she'd hardly seen for three years, and she would start her internship at the local newspaper. There were so many things to look forward to, and yet Ana knew the summer would not be as enjoyable as she had once hoped.

Ana had reasons to dread the summer. The family gathering would start out well, but it would end up being the same old drag. She would begin the day greeting people on the porch and sipping lemonade in the sun while she caught up with all her cousins, but the pleasantries wouldn't last. Somehow, she'd find herself stuck in the kitchen with her mother, sister, aunts, and grandmother, while her male cousins played baseball out back and her uncles sat drinking beer and laughing in the front yard. The sun would stream through the windows, steam would rise from the oven, and the kitchen would become an

unbearable sauna. As soon as the heat reached suffocating levels, Ana's grandmother would start in pummeling Ana with questions about boyfriends, religion, marriage, and children.

"So have you met any nice boys at that school of yours? What do you girls plan to do with all that education once you get married? Do they have churches in that college town? Now how do you plan to be a journalist and take care of your children?"

Ana would duck, swerve, and try to divert her grandmother's attention, but it would be to no avail. She would end up humming, hawing, and eventually lying. She'd have to. After all, what was she going to say? *Actually, Grandma, I've decided not to date for a few years. I don't know if I'll get married. Well, I really haven't had time to go to church. You know, I was thinking maybe I don't want children.*

No, Ana couldn't say these things. Her grandmother would clutch the cross dangling around her neck and call for Ana's grandfather. Ana's mother would yell, "Ana! Who taught you to talk like that? You want to give *Abuela* a heart attack? Go speak to your father!"

No, this could not happen. Peace in the family above all else—that's what Ana had been taught, and that's what she'd be forced to endure. And after it was all over, she'd visit her friends only to find that everything had changed. Teresa got married over Christmas. Concha had been married for two years already. Julia was going to have a baby. Clara worked all the time, and Eva, Ana's only close friend who had also gone to a four-year college, wasn't coming home because she was interning at a law firm in New York City for the summer. Of course, the remaining friends would go out, laugh, dance, and pretend that nothing had changed, but Ana knew there was no denying the different paths their lives had taken. Even worse, she sometimes got strange vibes from her friends and suspected they were whispering words like "traitor" and "sell-out"

behind her back. Ana feared that by summer's end, she'd feel more alone than ever.

In her book *Chiquita's Cocoon*, author Bettina R. Flores argues that the many positive aspects of Hispanic culture and tradition must be maintained but the hurtful, oppressive, and self-defeating aspects must be changed or cast off. Ana would probably agree with this statement. Ana, like many Hispanic women today, is struggling to balance her new opportunities and dreams with the conflicting messages she receives from some of her family. Furthermore, she is mourning the way her life path is carrying her farther away from childhood friends.

The difficulties Ana faces are by no means unique to Hispanic women. In fact, almost all young people experience some conflicts and confusion as they begin to establish lives and identities independent from their families. For some Hispanic women, however, family and cultural tradition will make these challenges more difficult to overcome.

HISPANIC WOMEN IN THE FAMILY

Today, Hispanic women occupy the same roles in their families as the ones they occupied in the past. Despite increased opportunities in education and the workforce, Hispanic women remain almost solely responsible for the daily cooking, cleaning, and maintenance of the household. Women also continue to be the caretakers of children and are generally expected to be obedient to and supportive of their husbands.

The trend for large families continues in Hispanic communities, although birth rates are generally lower than they used to be. According to the Centers for Disease Control and Prevention's 2002 study, Hispanic women in the United States have a *total fertility rate* of 3.1, well above the national average of

This little girl in Guatemala is already responsible for her baby brother's care.

2.1 births per woman. In other countries, these rates are even higher. Bolivia, Honduras, Nicaragua, and Paraguay, for example, all have total fertility rates above 3.5, and Guatemala has the highest rate in the Americas at 4.4. Furthermore, in Bolivia, Columbia, the Dominican Republic, and Nicaragua, more than one-quarter, and in Paraguay, more than one-third of all births occur within twenty-four months of the last pregnancy.

But what does a statistic like this tell us about women's lives? Well, for one, it helps us understand how many women are overwhelmed with childcare responsibilities. Infants and toddlers are completely dependent on their parents for their care, and are therefore much more demanding than older children who can be somewhat *self-sufficient*. When women have children close together, they are in the position of caring for two or more infants or toddlers at the same time—a highly demanding task that leaves women with little time or energy for anything else. Furthermore, when women have numerous pregnancies in a short period, they are less able to physically, emotionally, and financially recuperate between children.

To make matters more difficult, economic circumstances require that most women work outside of the home. This creates a double burden for women, because their responsibilities within the house do not decrease when they get jobs outside the home, since most men don't contribute to the household responsibilities. According to Flores, many parents still teach their daughters that "real life" starts with marriage and there is no option other than marriage. Furthermore, Flores echoes the American Association of University Women's assertion that women who want education and a career are sometimes chastised by their own families as turning their backs on their families, forgetting their roots, or trying to be Anglo.

Flores laments Hispanic women's continued subservient position within the home, but she also blames women for perpetuating some of the conditions and

Many modern Latina women are learning to interact with men as equals.

Women in Central America offer prayers at altars outside the church.

CULTURES UNDER THREAT?

When people think of a woman's role in the family, they often think of a woman cooking, cleaning, and balancing a baby on her hip. One of the most important functions that women have always played within their families and society, however, is cultural transmission—the passing on of beliefs, values, family history, and cultural practices from one generation to the next. Today, women's role in cultural transmission is more important than ever. Some members of the Hispanic community feel their culture is under threat. The culprit? "Americanization." In today's world of flashy advertising, new communication systems, technologies, and increased international contact, people see their children learning values from television, movies, magazines, and other sources—many of which come from America or are strongly influenced by American ideals. Sometimes these values contrast with their own beliefs. What some people see as great opportunities in today's world are for other people a cultural onslaught that threatens to destroy their long-held way of life.

attitudes that keep them subservient. She claims that both men and women still prefer boys over girls and that Hispanic mothers still pamper their sons but not their daughters. Flores believes that in providing this extra attention to their sons, Hispanic mothers teach boys to expect pampering from women; as adult males, they will tend to believe they have a right to special treatment. Flores asserts that if Hispanic women's position within the family is to improve, women need to be more *proactive* not only in teaching their daughters independence and self-sufficiency but also in teaching their sons about fairness and equality between the sexes.

As in times past, many Hispanic households are headed by women. This fact is explained by several factors, including: women in the Americas live about six years longer than men, and men abandon their families in greater numbers than women. Single-parent and female-headed households are more likely to face poverty than are two-parent or male-headed households. When husbands die or leave, women may be left with many children, no work experience, and few resources. Single-parent households only have one adult wage earner. Women who have only worked at home do not have their own pension plans, so if their husband dies, they may be left without financial support. Women who work outside the home also make less money than men. Factors like these contribute to higher poverty levels in female-headed households, and poverty remains a formidable problem for Hispanic communities.

DOMESTIC VIOLENCE IN HISPANIC FAMILIES

Another issue concerning Hispanic women's experiences within the family is domestic violence. Machismo, which we discussed in chapter 2, continues to influence Hispanic society, and some people feel it contributes to violence against women and children. Information collected from the United States Department of Justice shows that Hispanic women are less likely than white

Hispanic women in the United States are not always legal residents. If abuse occurs in their families, they are not likely to seek help from legal authorities for fear of being deported.

or black women to experience domestic violence. Hispanic culture's deep re-spect for women, particularly mothers, is often cited as a contributing factor to this lack of domestic abuse. However, other studies suggest that Hispanic women may face as much domestic violence as other women but are less likely to report that violence or admit it to anyone, even within their own families.

What would lead Hispanic women to be so silent on such an important and potentially life-threatening issue? Scholars speculate that Hispanic culture's huge emphasis on personal and familial honor keeps women silent. In a society that values honor so highly, many women are taught and believe that it is better to endure their suffering in silence than to bring shame to their husbands and families. In cases of physical abuse, women are expected to "bear their cross" like a "good wife," a concept with decidedly religious overtones.

Other circumstances might also cause Hispanic women to remain silent in the face of domestic violence. In the case of immigrants, women may not report violence to legal authorities because they are afraid that they or their partners will be *deported*, especially if they are illegal immigrants. Furthermore, in the United States, the typical approach to ending domestic violence is to separate the partners, help the abused person become independent and self-sufficient, and prosecute the abuser in court. A recent study based on interviews with Hispanic women about domestic violence found that the Hispanic women interviewed were less likely than women of other groups to want to leave their relationship or see their abuser punished. Many Hispanic women say they want the violence to end but the relationship to continue, something that the current system is ill-equipped to *facilitate*.

There are numerous groups, such as the Latino Alliance for the Elimination of Domestic Violence, trying to combat domestic violence within Hispanic society by developing new approaches, services, and options for families in crisis. One program that attempts to combat domestic violence in a new way is El Hombre Noble (The Noble Man). In this program, instead of removing abused women from their homes, violent men enter an education program. The pro-

gram is a type of reeducation about what it means to be a man and how men can become positive forces in their families' lives. The hope is that through programs like these, women who would otherwise not report domestic violence for fear of losing their families will be able to live improved, safer lives with their partners.

"HOW NATURAL THAT THE ERRORS OF THE ANCIENT SHOULD BE HANDED DOWN AND, MIXING WITH THE PRINCIPLES AND SYSTEM WHICH CHRIST TAUGHT, GIVE US AN ADULTERATED CHRISTIANITY."
—OLYMPIA BROWN

RELIGIOUS INFLUENCES
ON HISPANIC WOMEN'S LIVES

Throughout this book we have mentioned a number of cultural beliefs and practices, like women's obedience to their husbands and tendency to have many children, that are related to religious values. Indeed, religion plays an extremely important role in most Hispanic people's lives, and religious values tend to have an especially large influence in the familial and economic spheres.

The vast majority of Hispanic people are Catholic. Catholicism is a Christian religion, and Christian religions are based on the belief that the Jewish teacher, Jesus of Nazareth, was the Son of God. According to Christianity, Jesus was sent to earth as a sacrifice to redeem the human race from its sins so that humans could once again reside with God in heaven. Spanish missionaries brought Christianity to the Americas in the form of Roman Catholicism, a highly organized Christian religion whose teachings are handed down from the head of the church, the Pope, in Rome.

Christianity is a religion that takes many different forms throughout the world. Different local practices and beliefs are often absorbed into Christianity, and Christian religions can vary greatly from place to place.

For example, one of the ways in which Catholicism is practiced in Hispanic culture is through the home *shrine*. Many Hispanic families, especially of the older generations, will keep a place in their home as a shrine to one of the saints, most often the Virgin Mary. According to Catholic belief, some human beings live such exemplary lives that God chooses to work through them on earth. God may work through these special people to perform miracles, heal the

Today, though the vast majority of Hispanic people are still Christian, religions other than Catholicism are growing in popularity. Three of the fastest growing Christian religions among the Hispanic community are the Baptist, Pentecostal, and Mormon religions.

The Catholic churches in Peru are filled with gold.

sick, give aid to the suffering, teach the masses, or do other religious work. Catholics believe that when these saints die, they occupy a privileged position in heaven and can speak to God on behalf of living people. You can think of this a little like going to court. If you decide to represent yourself in a court case, you might not make out so well. If you have a lawyer to speak to the judge for you, you'll probably have a better case. The position of a saint in heaven could be seen as similar to the position of a lawyer in a courtroom. Many Hispanic

In Olympia Brown's quote at the beginning of this chapter, it is clear that she thinks Christianity became corrupted over time. There are many scholars who would agree with her and who believe Christianity's attitudes toward women are actually a distortion of Christ's original teachings. Today, archeologists are still uncovering ancient materials that recorded early Christian teachings and contributed to the formation of the Christian Bible. Some of these materials suggest that Jesus saw women as men's equals, and women were among Jesus' first followers and apostles.

households will have a shrine to a specific saint, a place of honor where prayers can be offered up and requests made for the saint to *intercede* on the person's behalf. Home shrines, however, are not common in non-Hispanic Catholic communities.

Many of the ways in which Christianity affects a woman's life have as much to do with the way Christianity has adapted to her particular culture's belief systems as to specific teachings within the Bible. According to some interpretations of the Christian Bible, women should obey their husbands, both men and women should be virtuous and without sin, and both men and women should abstain from sexual relations before marriage. Like Hispanic culture in general, Catholicism requires obedience from women.

In chapter 2, we discussed machismo and its affect on Hispanic culture. In their book *Modern Latin America*, Thomas E. Skidmore and Peter H. Smith describe a female counterpart to machismo called *marianismo*. Whereas machismo is the cultivation of "male qualities" in men, marianismo is the cultivation in women of the "female qualities" associated with the Virgin Mary. The Catholic religion reveres Mary, the mother of Jesus Christ, as an example for all women. According to the Catholic religion, Mary was a woman of purity, patience, humility, and self-sacrifice. A woman who could *emulate* all these qualities in her own life would have marianismo. Marianismo also encourages the subjugation, subservience, and inferior status of women in Hispanic society.

As with machismo, it would be wrong to stereotype all Hispanic women as having or desiring marianismo. And the Catholic religion can be an important source of strength and comfort for women enduring hard times.

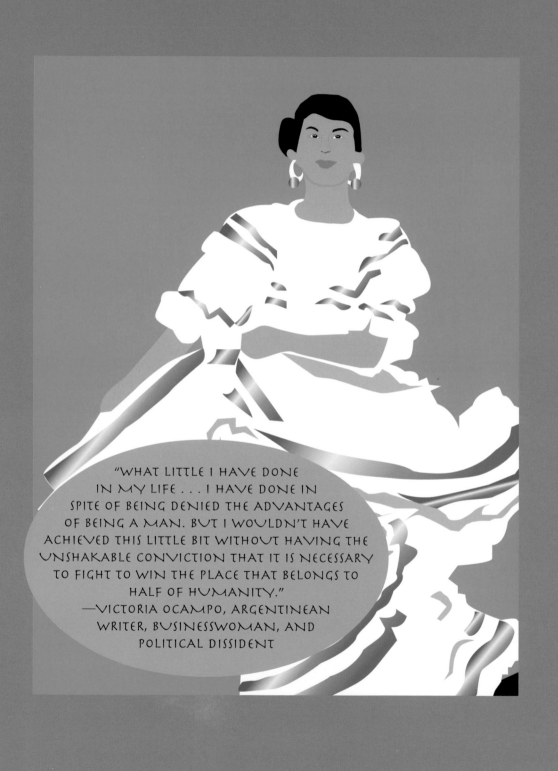

"WHAT LITTLE I HAVE DONE
IN MY LIFE . . . I HAVE DONE IN
SPITE OF BEING DENIED THE ADVANTAGES
OF BEING A MAN. BUT I WOULDN'T HAVE
ACHIEVED THIS LITTLE BIT WITHOUT HAVING THE
UNSHAKABLE CONVICTION THAT IT IS NECESSARY
TO FIGHT TO WIN THE PLACE THAT BELONGS TO
HALF OF HUMANITY."
—VICTORIA OCAMPO, ARGENTINEAN
WRITER, BUSINESSWOMAN, AND
POLITICAL DISSIDENT

THE STUFF OF MYTHS AND LEGENDS: HISPANIC WOMEN WHO HAVE CHANGED THE WORLD

No book about women in Hispanic society could be complete without talking about some of the individual women who have influenced that society. Those women are countless and come from every corner of the Spanish-speaking world. Some are legends of the past. Others are just beginning their work. All give glimpses of the great variety of talents and contributions Hispanic women have made to the world. Here are the stories of just a few of these great women.

EVA PERÓN

Born in Argentina in 1919, Eva María Ibarguren was the youngest of five children. She never knew her father; he was not married to Eva's mother and in fact had a different wife and family. When Eva was just one year old, her father decided to return to this other family, leaving Eva's mother penniless. Eva's mother worked as a seamstress to make ends meet, but the family never recovered from the abandonment or the insults they suffered in their small town. Other than sparse details like these, however, we know very little about Eva's

Eva Perón

young life. After all, no one was expecting this poor and seemingly unremarkable little girl to become one of the most influential women the Western Hemisphere has ever seen.

Many sources say Eva left her family when she was just ten years old, but like so many other stories about Eva's life, this is probably a myth. According to Nicholas Fraser and Marysa Navarro, authors of *Evita: The Real Life of Eva Perón*, Eva probably left home at fifteen. After living a childhood of poverty and scorn, she dreamed of better things and was fiercely determined to get them. But how could a poor girl from a despised family make it in the world? She had only a basic education, no financial resources, and no connections. What she had an endless supply of, however, was ambition. She decided to become an actress in the big city: Buenos Aires.

Eva Duarte—she now used her father's surname for fear the label *illegitimate* would stalk her throughout her life—endured a number of lean and humiliating years. She rented cheap rooms, went hungry, and found little work. Some of the more successful actors laughed at her ambition, declared her talentless, and even proclaimed her ugly. As most other struggling actresses did, Eva relied on boyfriends and relationships to get her through the hard times.

Living in the big city, however, taught Eva about *deportment*, fashion, and beauty. Eva, the poor girl from the country, cultivated a fashionable appearance and urban style. She found success, not in film or theatre, but in radio, where she began a triumphant climb up the ladder of sought-after actresses. Her big break came when she proposed and got approval for a series called "Heroines of History," in which she portrayed the lives of historic women. The series was a hit. People finally noticed Eva, and Eva could now call herself a star.

This success, however, would pale in comparison to what came next. In a benefit function for earthquake victims, Eva met the Secretary of Labour, Colonel Juan Domingo Perón. Although the Ministry of Labour may not have seemed very important to some people, through its work, Perón was becoming the most powerful man in Argentina. That night, Perón and Eva left the benefit together, and soon Eva was a constant at Perón's side.

Eva fell quickly and deeply in love with Perón and became his biggest supporter. She moved into his apartment, began a political radio broadcast that declared Perón a savior of the working-class people, and maintained a quiet, background presence at the nightly meetings held at the apartment. In the nightly meetings, Eva behaved more like a maid than a political adviser. She served refreshments and lingered in the shadows. In this silent role, however, she analyzed those present and determined who Perón could and could not trust.

Perón's behavior infuriated many people. At that time in Argentina, unmarried people did not live together, women did not participate in politics, and no one broke social conventions so *brazenly* and unapologetically. Rumors circulated that Eva was a prostitute. Even Perón's supporters protested by gathering in front of the apartment and chanting "Get married!" Perón and Eva, however, were completely unrepentant and showed no sign of adjusting their lifestyle.

On October 9, 1945, the axe fell for Perón and Eva. The army command was fed up with the couple's behavior and political maneuvering. In an interview for *Evita: The Real Life of Eva Perón*, General Gerardo Demetro later said, "We were convinced that it was our duty to stop the nation from falling into the hands of that woman, as in fact ultimately happened." The army informed Argentina's president that if Perón wasn't forced to resign, the army would lead a *coup* against the government. Perón immediately resigned. Across town, Eva was fired from the radio station.

Perón, however, did not leave quietly. The next morning, with 15,000 of his supporters (including Eva) gathered in the streets, Perón gave a speech that would change the course of Argentina's history. The speech was mainly to announce his resignation, but in so doing, Perón also announced his final act before leaving office: approving a general wage increase and other measures that would safeguard workers' earnings. The nationally broadcast speech brought a

WOMEN IN THE HISPANIC WORLD

These Hispanic women from Cuba will never be as famous as Eva Perón—but they are still proud of their achievements.

new wave of support for Perón. It also further enflamed the rage of those who hated him. Death threats were made, and members of the army called for Perón's arrest. Soon, Eva and Perón were on the run. Within days, Perón was arrested, and Eva was left frightened and alone.

Many accounts give Eva complete credit for what happened next, but in reality, she probably played only a small role. She did attempt, but failed, to secure Perón's release, and she contacted supporters and tried to get information on his condition. She could not, however, have organized the inexplicable events in Argentina. Workers were walking off their jobs and taking to the streets. People who had never been loyal to Perón before were suddenly *invoking* his name. Unions feared that, with Perón gone from the Ministry of Labour, they would lose the gains made under him. A general strike was planned for October 17, but by October 16, thousands of people had gathered, shut down the capital, and were chanting Perón's name. That evening, having seen the country so suddenly and unexpectedly descend into chaos and not knowing what else to do, the government released Perón. The crowd went crazy when Perón stepped onto the platform to address them. The ovation lasted fifteen minutes before he could speak at all. The next day, instead of leaving their jobs as strikers, the workers walked off the jobs as celebrants in what would become a national holiday.

In the following weeks, Perón and Eva married, and Perón began his campaign for the presidency of Argentina. Despite now having a "legitimate" relationship, Eva continued to upset people. She acted as no Argentine woman had before. She worked on Perón's campaign, stood beside him while he made speeches, expressed her opinions openly, and gave direction to campaign workers—none of which endeared Eva to the men working for Perón. This did not, however, diminish his support among the working-class people. When Eva leaned from the campaign train to touch the followers who reached for her hands, she even enhanced that support, and in a surprising victory, Perón was elected president. At just twenty-six, Eva Perón was now the president's wife.

The elite of Argentina had hated Eva from the day she set foot on the political scene, but to the masses, hers was a rags-to-riches fairytale. Any newspaper or magazine bearing her picture flew off the shelves. People could not get

WOMEN IN THE HISPANIC WORLD

A Latina woman with her own style of glamour.

enough of their blond-haired, flamboyantly dressed first lady. She took a three-month tour of Europe in which the world press got its first good look at the woman many called by the pet name Evita.

When she returned home, she declared her love for Perón and Perón's love for the people wherever she went. After women were granted the right to vote, she created a Women's Party, the members of which became fiercely loyal to Perón. Eva developed into a powerfully emotional orator, and swept Perón's movement into near-cult hero-worship.

Soon Eva's political work took on a new obsession. Although she was not an official employee of the government, she kept an office at the Ministry of Labour. People in need lined up to tell her their troubles, and she used her influence to secure aid for them. With the founding of the Eva Perón Foundation, however, this charitable work became a personal *crusade*. The foundation, aided by government grants, union donations, and personal contributions (aid that was not always freely given, for businesses could find themselves shut down if they did not support the foundation), built homes; purchased medicine; gave money, sewing machines, clothing, shoes, food; and provided any number of services to the poor. Each day, people flooded the ministry to see Eva, and she met them all personally, often returning home well after midnight to get only a few hours rest before returning to work. Through her foundation, she started a training school for nurses and built twelve state-of-the-art hospitals to serve the poor. She organized for every village in the country to start a soccer team, gave these teams equipment, and then used the teams as a vehicle for social services. Health workers arrived at the soccer matches to give the children medical exams and to investigate their family and school situations. The foundation also built one thousand schools, ran four nursing homes, and converted four blocks of Buenos Aires into a "Children's City" where needy children came for help, housing, and education. Through this work, Eva became as important to the "New Argentina" as Perón was, and in the next election, Perón's supporters called for Eva to stand as the vice presidential candidate.

Eva Perón would never receive this honor. Though the huge outpouring of public support for her candidacy shocked everyone with its magnitude (perhaps even Eva herself), a woman in such an important position was unacceptable to

WOMEN IN THE HISPANIC WORLD

those in power, including Perón. Eva's inability to run for the vice presidency was a great disappointment to herself and to Perón's supporters, but it soon became irrelevant. Eva had been showing signs of illness for months. She had grown steadily thinner and paler. She ate less, slept less, and had pain in her abdomen. For months, those around Eva blamed her condition on overwork, but shortly after the scandal involving her possible run for the vice presidency, it became clear to everyone that Eva Perón was not simply sick. She was dying.

ISABEL MARTÍNEZ DE PERÓN

Juan Perón later regained the presidency of Argentina, and his third wife, Isabel Martínez de Perón, gained, almost effortlessly, what Eva Perón dreamed but never received: the vice presidency of Argentina. Barely two months after being reelected president, Perón died suddenly of a heart attack, and the male-dominated government's worst dream came true: a woman succeeded to the presidency. Isabel's presidency, however, did not last long. She had no experience in politics and lacked Eva's power with the masses. She was forced out of power after two years.

Although no one ever told Eva the name of the disease from which she suffered, she had advanced uterine cancer—the same disease that had killed Perón's first wife years before. Perón won reelection, but within a year, thirty-three-year-old Eva Perón was dead.

When the news hit the streets, Argentina descended into deep mourning. In the capital, all businesses closed, people gathered around the president's residence to pray, and mourners began piling flowers at the Ministry of Labour. The next day, lines stretched literally for miles as people gathered to view their heroine's body. Over the next thirteen days, the steady stream of mourners continued unabated.

Today, Eva Perón's true life is difficult to distinguish from the great *mythology* that arose after her death. Both her good works and her faults have been so exaggerated by those who loved her and those who hated her that few have been able to give a fair account of this historic woman's life. Shortly after Eva's death, Perón was forced from power, and those who had opposed Perónism, as his political movement came to be known, hid Eva's body and set about dismantling her foundation and most of her work. Despite their efforts to wipe Eva from the pages of history, her legend continued to grow. By the end of her life, Eva Perón had become nearly a *demigod* of the people, and after her death, Evita became immortal.

FRIDA KAHLO

Born in Mexico City in 1907, Frida Kahlo, like many people who today would be labeled "Hispanic," had a mixed heritage. Her mother was Spanish and Mexican Indian. Her father was Hungarian Jewish, had been born in Germany, and immigrated to Mexico. By all accounts, Frida was a boisterous, mischievous child. Frida's mother was quite traditional and believed in women's roles of the period. Frida's father, however, saw no reason why Frida should be confined to the world of kitchen and home. His encouragement was an important influence

WOMEN IN THE HISPANIC WORLD

Frida Kahlo

Frida Kahlo's studio in Mexico City.

in young Frida's development. Even he, however, would have never dreamed that his daughter would become one of the most important artists of the twentieth century.

Frida's father was one of Mexico's *preeminent* photographers of the time, so art had been present in Frida's life from the beginning. She personally, however, showed no signs in her early years of the artist she would become. In fact, her original ambition was to become a doctor. Perhaps it was her childhood battle with polio that initiated her interest in medicine. She survived the disease that killed so many children of her time, but one of her legs was left permanently smaller than the other.

Frida had been extremely lucky. The condition, though permanent, was not seriously debilitating. To aid her recuperation, Frida's father suggested she play active sports and games despite the fact these were not "traditional" pastimes for girls. She recovered well, and though she had fallen somewhat behind her peers during her illness, when she was just fifteen years old, she began training in a premedical program.

Frida would never become a doctor. Three years after her premedical training began, a horrible bus accident forever changed the course and quality of her life. Few thought Frida could survive the physical trauma of the event. She was impaled on an iron rod. Her foot was crushed. Her right leg was fractured in eleven places. Her pelvis, spine, collarbone, and some ribs were all broken. She had emergency surgery and woke up to find herself trapped within a full-body cast. Though the odds were stacked against her, Frida survived. She was, however, in tremendous and constant pain. As the months of recuperation dragged on, depression and boredom mixed with her physical discomfort. Able to do little else, Frida picked up a brush and began teaching herself to paint. It was a move that would change her life and greatly influence modern art.

From that day forward, painting would be a type of therapy for Frida. She always painted alone, and dreamlike self-portraits—portraits that often pictured a

woman in desperate pain—became her trademark. As many of her paintings would suggest, Frida was in pain nearly all of the time. Though she miraculously recovered and even regained the ability to walk, the pain never left her. She would undergo more than thirty-five operations in less than thirty years. Despite her pain and numerous medical complications, to her friends, Frida was always a picture of life and defiance. Something of the mischievous young Frida never faded and showed herself in Frida's distinctive clothing, ready humor, uninhibited drinking, and clear sensuality.

If the bus accident was the greatest event to shape Frida's adult life, then Diego Rivera was the greatest person to influence Frida. Rivera was a prominent artist who had already received worldwide attention. He and his art were also highly political, and he was the founder of the Young Communist League, which Frida joined. This was not, however, the first time she met Rivera. She had first seen the great artist years before when he was painting a mural for her school. They now began a passionate relationship. Frida was twenty-two when they married. Diego Rivera was forty-two.

Frida's artwork continued to develop in vivid colors, tortured characters, and bizarre depictions. Her paintings dealt with images and themes never before seen in the art world. Some called her a *surrealist,* but Frida vehemently insisted that she painted her reality. Frida and Diego were now moving in the most important art and political circles in the world of that time. Pablo Picasso was reportedly an admirer of Frida's work. Russian revolutionary Leon Trotsky sought *asylum* in Mexico and lived for a time with Rivera and Kahlo.

The marriage, however, was not a happy one. At times, Diego and Frida seemed to only wish to hurt each other. They had numerous affairs and were separated, divorced, and then remarried. Perhaps more painful than this for Frida were her numerous miscarriages. The injuries she suffered in the bus accident made it impossible for Frida to have children, a fact she would never fully accept.

One of the most amazing and influential Hispanic women working in activism today is Dolores Fernández Huerta. Born in 1930, Huerta worked with famous activist and labor-leader César Chavez to organize the United Farm Workers, gain passage of the Agricultural Labor Relations Act, and secure greater rights for farm workers. After Chavez's death, Huerta carried on this important fight, becoming one of the most experienced leaders of nonviolent protest movements and important civil rights activists in the United States. In 1988, she was nearly killed by police officers during a peaceful demonstration against then future-president George Bush's policies. She recovered, however, from her ruptured spleen, broken ribs, and emergency surgery and continues her activist work today.

Perhaps the greatest injustice of Frida's life, however, was the fact that few people truly appreciated her artwork and its importance until after she died. Frida had never been one to pay much attention to *social sanctions* or care about gender norms; nevertheless, many people always saw Frida simply as Diego

Rivera's wife, the flamboyantly dressed little woman who dabbled in painting while the great artist created his masterpieces.

In 1954, at the age of forty-seven, Frida died. The previous year, her right leg had been amputated due to gangrene, and deep depression and suicidal feelings marked many of her final days. Some rumored that she committed suicide. Others say she finally succumbed to the medical complications that plagued her for three decades. Although some people would not realize it for many years, one thing happened for certain that day: the world lost one of its most important and revolutionary artists—the independent Frida Kahlo, who in her life and her works created an artistic world that was all her own.

Of course we do not have time here to review all the amazing Hispanic women who have ever lived, but from just these few examples, you can see that women play a vital role in their communities and in the world. Throughout history and even today, women's work and influence have gone unrecognized or been underappreciated, but this does not diminish their abilities or importance. In the Spanish-speaking countries of the Americas, women have been wives, mothers, businesswomen, leaders, warriors, saints, artists, scientists, authors, and every other occupation known to humankind. Their proud legacy lives on in the Hispanic women of today. Buoyed by new opportunities in education, employment, and government, their heritage will continue to increase tomorrow.

FURTHER READING

Chambers, Veronica. *Quinceañera Means Sweet 15*. New York: Hyperion Books for Children, 2001.

Flores, Bettina R. *Chiquita's Cocoon*. Granite Bay, Calif.: Pepper Vine Press, 1990.

Fox, Geoffrey. *Hispanic Nation: Culture, Politics, and the Construction of Identity*. Tucson, Ariz.: The University of Arizona Press, 1996.

Fraser, Nicholas and Marysa Navarro. *Evita: The Real Life of Eva Perón*. New York: W. W. Norton, 1996.

The Latina Feminist Group, ed. *Telling to Live: Latina Feminist Testimonios*. Durham, N.C.: Duke University Press, 2001.

Morrison, Andrew R. *Too Close to Home: Domestic Violence in Latin America*. Washington, D.C.: Inter-American Development Bank, 1999.

Nickles, Greg. *We Came to North America: The Hispanics*. New York: Crabtree, 2001.

Osa, Nancy. *Cuba 15: A Novel*. New York: Delacorte Press, 2003.

Sinnott, Susan. *Extraordinary Hispanic Americans*. Chicago, Ill.: Children's Press, 1991.

Skidmore, Thomas E., and Peter H. Smith. *Modern Latin America*. New York: Oxford University Press, 2001.

Sullivan, Charles, ed. *Here is My Kingdom: Hispanic-American Literature and Art for Young People*. New York: Harry N. Abrams, 1994.

FOR MORE INFORMATION

Advancing Women: Hispanic Women—Latinas on the Rise
www.advancingwomen.com/hispanic.html

Congresswoman Linda Sanchez's Web site
www.house.gov/lindasanchez

Congresswoman Loretta Sanchez's Web site
www.lorettasanchez.house.gov

Hispanic Online's Hispanic Heritage Plaza 2002
www.hispaniconline.com/hh02/education_celeb_hisp_heritage.html

Las Mujeres: Information on notable Latin women
www.lasmujeres.com

Latina Style.com: A National Magazine for the Contemporary Hispanic Woman
www.latinastyle.com

MANA®: A National Latina Organization
www.hermana.org

National Hispanic Cultural Center
www.nhccnm.org

National Women's Hall of Fame
www.greatwomen.org

The Pan American Health Organization's Gender, Health, and Development
in the Americas 2003
www.paho.org/English/DPM/GPP/GH/GenderBrochure.pdf

¡Soy Unica! ¡Soy Latina! Bilingual Web site
www.soyunica.gov

The United Nations
www.un.org

WomenWatch: Information and Resources on Gender Equality
and Empowerment of Women
www.un.org/womenwatch/asp/user/list.asp?ParentID=20

Zona Latina: Latin American Media & Marketing
www.zonalatina.com

Publisher's note:
The Web sites listed on these pages were active at the time of publication. The
publisher is not responsible for Web sites that have changed their addresses or
discontinued operation since the date of publication. The publisher will review
and update the Web sites upon each reprint.

GLOSSARY

accessible Approachable, able to achieve.

activists People who take action on behalf of a cause.

advocate To speak and act on behalf of something or someone.

Anglos Belonging to a white inhabitant of the United States, not of Hispanic descent.

assertiveness Having a self-confident attitude.

asylum A place of safety.

atrocities Things that are extremely wicked, brutal, or cruel.

brazenly In a brash, loud, bold manner.

civil Relating to the state and its citizens.

cohesive Exhibiting the ability to join and stay together.

conquistadors Leaders in the Spanish conquest of America.

correlation A relationship between things or events.

coup The sudden, often unexpected overthrow of a government.

cross-culturally To relate to people of different beliefs and behaviors than oneself.

crusade An action taken with much enthusiasm and zeal.

cultural Relating to the customary beliefs and traits of a racial, religious, or social group.

demigod A mythological creature with more power than a human but less than possessed by a god.

deported Forced by legal action to leave a country, often because it has been entered illegally.

deportment The manner in which one behaves.

discrimination Treating someone differently than others, often of the basis of gender of skin color.

disparity The difference between things.

dissidence Disagreement.

dissolution Separate, end.

diverse Having different qualities.

emulate To act like, or take on the characteristics of another.

entrepreneurs People who take on the responsibilities, management, and risks of a business.

ethnicity One's racial, tribal, national, religious, linguistic, or cultural background.

facilitate To make something easier to happen.

first-generation The first children of immigrant parents.

grassroots The most basic, common level.

illegitimate Born of parents who are not married.

individualism Characteristics that are specific to that person.

intercede Act on the behalf of another.

invoking Appealing to someone for help or assistance.

Latin America All of the Americas south of the United States.

leniency The state of having a soothing or easing manner.

linguistic Relating to language.

literacy The ability to read and write.

media modes Of mass communication including television, radio, and newspapers.

mythology A body of beliefs dealing with gods, demigods, and heroes.

parliament A governing body.

perpetuated Allowed to continue.

persona The personality a person projects in public.

preeminent To stand out, have the highest quality.

prestige One's standing in the eyes of others.

proactive To act before something happens.

protectorate A country or people that is dependent on a more powerful country or group of people.

racist One who believes that genetic breeding (race) is the determinant of superiority.

sanctioned To have official approval.

self-sufficient To be able to maintain oneself without the help of others.

shantytown A poor section of town consisting mostly of crude dwellings.

shrine A place where devotion is paid to a saint or god.

social sanctions approval or disapproval by society.

stereotypes Beliefs based on information about a few but generalized toward many; they are often prejudiced.

subjugation The placing of someone under the control of another.

subservient Being useful in an inferior position.

surrealist An artist with subjects having unusual or fantastic relationships and characteristics.

total fertility rate The average number of babies born to women during their reproductive years.

INDEX

PICTURE CREDITS

Artville: p. 6; Michelle Bouch: pp. 60, 64, 88, 97; Corbis: pp. 39, 40, 43, 44, 51, 52, 55, 71; Corel: cover, pp. 18, 27, 28, 31, 73, 74, 77, 83, 98; Viola Gommer: p. 91; Hollingsworth: pp. 17, 22, 25; Map Resources: cover; Photos.com: pp. 13, 14, 32, 34, 55, 59, 68, 93; Rubberball: cover; Benjamin Stewart: cover.

BIOGRAPHIES

Autumn Libal is a freelance author and illustrator living in Vancouver, British Columbia. She received her degree from Smith College, an all women's college in Northampton, Massachusetts, where she developed a deep interest in women's issues. Autumn's writing has also appeared in *New Moon: The Magazine for Girls and Their Dreams,* as well as other Mason Crest series including, NORTH AMERICAN FOLKLORE and NORTH AMERICAN INDIANS TODAY.

Dr. Mary Jo Dudley is the director of Cornell University's Gender and Global Change Department, which focuses on the evolving role of gender around the world. She is also the associate director of Latin American Studies at Cornell.